THE FALL OF THE MONGOL EMPIRE

DISINTEGRATION, DISEASE, AND AN ENDURING LEGACY

THE MONGOLS™

THE FALL OF THE MONGOL EMPIRE

DISINTEGRATION, DISEASE, AND AN ENDURING LEGACY

JENNIFER SWANSON

ROSEN
PUBLISHING®

New York

Published in 2017 by The Rosen Publishing Group, Inc.
29 East 21st Street, New York, NY 10010

Library of Congress Cataloging-in-Publication Data

Names: Swanson, Jennifer, author.
Title: The fall of the Mongol empire : disintegration, disease, and an enduring legacy / Jennifer Swanson.
Description: First edition. | New York, NY : Rosen Publishing, 2017. | Series: The Mongols | Includes bibliographical references and index. | Audience: Grade 7 to 12.
Identifiers: LCCN 2015047631| ISBN 9781499463767 (library bound) | ISBN 9781499463743 (pbk.) | ISBN 9781499463750 (6-pack)
Subjects: LCSH: Mongols--History--To 1500.
Classification: LCC DS19 .S93 2016 | DDC 950/.2--dc23
LC record available at http://lccn.loc.gov/2015047631

Manufactured in China

CONTENTS

INTRODUCTION

The Mongol Empire was one of the largest dynasties in the world. At the height of its power, the empire stretched across Asia and into eastern Europe. That is an area of between 11,000 and 12,000 miles (17,703 and 19,312 kilometers). It is as big as the whole continent of Africa! The man behind its creation was Temujin, better known as Genghis Khan. Over the span of twenty years, Genghis Khan led his one hundred thousand troops on a mission to conquer almost 20 percent of the world. He united all of the nomadic tribes under one rule. After Genghis Khan's death in 1227, his legacy was carried on by his sons and grandsons. Their combined efforts resulted in a single empire that ruled almost one hundred million people.

Scholars debate the legacy of the Mongols. On one side, the Mongols have a reputation for being strict rulers. Some even consider them to be barbaric. The leaders of the Mongol Empire were focused only on securing new land and peoples. They were ruthless, sometimes destroying everything and everyone in their path. Other scholars argue that the harsh administration of peace promoted trade between countries. The Mongols established the Yassa, a set of laws to govern the empire. These laws kept trade routes safe. Merchants and ships from across Asia and Europe could safely sell and exchange goods.

Ships like these, known as cogs, carried cargo of animals, furs, tea, silk, and cloth for trade between Asia and Europe.

The legacy of the Mongol Empire can also be seen in the extensive mixture of culture and religions. The open trade routes allowed people from many different cultures to criss-cross Asia. Kublai Khan, a grandson of Genghis Khan and one of the supreme rulers of the empire, was responsible for promoting tolerance. He invited and often sought out different cultures and religions to thrive within his capital city. His open-ness to new ideas helped to expand the religions of Islam, Christianity, and Buddhism. Mongols had a strict sense of loyalty and honor. They respected these qualities, even in their enemies. Many of the Mongolian tribes were literate, meaning they kept written records of their occurrences.

As spectacular as its creation was, the fall of the Mongol Empire was just as remarkable. Its descent into chaos was sig-naled by interfamily rebellion. Upon the death of Kublai Khan, the empire was ruled by many weak leaders. They fought with each other in order to establish their authority. None was ever able to reunite the entire empire. Natural disasters brought about drought, flood, and famine. The bubonic plague began along the Silk Road and spread throughout the empire. It dev-astated populations in both Asia and Europe.

Ultimately the dynasty broke apart and was overthrown. Hundreds of years later, the legacy of the Mongols remains. It is visible in China, Russia, and eastern Europe. The empire has been credited with creating lines of communication and trade that led to an increase in science, the arts, and technol-ogy. The influence of the Mongol Empire, the largest in history, lives on.

Chapter 1
The Beginning of the End

It is difficult to pinpoint the actual time that the Mongol Empire began its decline. Some scholars say it happened when Genghis Khan died. Genghis Khan split his kingdom into four different regions. He called them khanates. The individual khanates, however, remained strong. They were again somewhat united under Kublai Khan. Upon the death of Kublai Khan, the Mongol Empire lost its power to act as a unified dynasty. The four khanates were ruled independently and were full of internal conflict.

The Rise of Genghis Khan

Early people of Mongolia were nomads. They roamed about the country in tribes, living and working the land. Initially, the Mongolian people were mixed with the Turks, who ruled the area, creating a Turko-Mongolian culture. Life in the steppes, or unforested grasslands, was not easy. The harsh climate and lack of water made growing crops and keeping animals difficult. The Mongols were briefly united under Kabul Khan, in the early 1100s, but that did not last long. By 1160, the Mongols had separated once again into tribes. These tribes warred constantly with each other. Such was the state of the empire until Genghis Khan began his ascent to power in the early thirteenth century.

The Mongol army was well known and feared for their brutal tactics. These warriors were especially effective on horseback, which allowed them to move quickly and surprise their opponents.

Genghis Khan merged the different nomadic tribes by combat on horseback. His soldiers were very skilled in riding horses. They also excelled at archery, hand-to-hand combat, and the armored lance. Genghis Khan demanded strict loyalty from his soldiers. He did not allow destruction of cities or towns without his permission. The well-trained army led by Genghis Khan swept through Asia like a rising storm, overtaking everything in its path. Their tactics on horseback included a head-on strike to the center of the opposition. The enemies would scatter. Then the Mongol army would chase them down and kill them. Genghis Khan was a brutal leader, and his armies could be

The Mongols, while brutal, did not allow enslavement of other Mongols, something that under tribal law had previously been acceptable. They did, however, sometimes enslave people from China or other conquered territories.

ruthless. They slaughtered countless tribes, including women and children. It was their way to gain control of the land. People were so afraid of the army that whole groups would sometimes surrender, simply to avoid being defeated.

While seen as a bloodthirsty horde, the Mongols actually preferred surrender to mass destruction. Those cities or towns that surrendered willingly, however, were treated with compassion. The leaders of the city were left in place, and the land remained unchanged. This was fine with Genghis Khan, provided the city was willing to accept the rule of Mongol law. If the city rebelled, its entire population was destroyed. Many towns felt

THE QANAT

The underground irrigation system, called the qanat, consisted of large, sloping tunnels that funneled water from an underground river to the dry steppe region.

Genghis Khan had little regard for the land itself. The steppe region was very dry. Water needed for farming came from an irrigation system known as the qanat. The qanat required regular maintenance. Farmers had to continuously dig out the trenches to prevent them from silting up. That means the dirt from the sides of the trench would fall into the water. This would cause the water to slow down. If this was not done, the trenches would stop up. When the Mongol army invaded a region, the people fled, leaving the trenches unattended. The result was a lack of water that caused farms to quite literally dry up and leave people without food.

that accepting the invading Mongol army was the better choice. The result was that in fewer than twenty-five years, the Mongol army had extended its empire across the entire continent of Asia and part of eastern Europe.

Mongol law was often brutal. It supported swift judgment when laws were broken. On the other hand, the strict Mongol laws, known as the Yassa, also benefited the people. It was against the law to enslave another Mongol. It was also illegal to kidnap and sell women or to steal livestock. These decrees had never existed before under tribal laws. They helped to maintain order within the towns. The sense of honor and integrity of the Mongols was well known across the world.

PAX MONGOLICA

One of the most significant legacies of Genghis Khan's reign is the Pax Mongolica, or Mongol peace. It occurred under the rule of Kublai Khan, grandson of Genghis Khan. It established peace along the trade route, known as the Silk Road. This made communication, trade, and exchange of ideas much easier. It was

LINES OF COMMUNICATION

The Mongol Empire set up the first structured communication system. It was very difficult for Genghis Khan to keep in touch with his generals across the vast Mongol Empire. To improve communication, he established an "arrow messenger" system. The messengers rode on horseback from station to station to carry messages and official written mail across the empire. This kept Genghis Khan informed of the happenings within the empire.

The postal system was known as the Yam. It was one of the legacies that the Mongol Empire left to the whole of Asia. During times of peace, a letter could be transported from one end of the empire to another in about one month.

illegal to attack any officials, military men, or tradesmen traveling the route. These men carried passports, or papers, to show their identity. The promise of safe travel encouraged many to set out for new areas of the empire, which in turn allowed for a mix of many different cultures. The routes spanned thousands of miles and connected the major centers of commercial goods from Asia to central Europe.

Genghis Khan was the leader of one of the most powerful armies in the world. When he died in 1227, the Mongol Empire was more than double the size of the Roman Empire. He conquered twice as much land as anyone had previously. He was responsible for bringing the eastern and western civilizations into contact with each other. Genghis Khan's single-minded determination to unite a continent had paid off. He had cemented his place in the history of the world, but how long would it last?

Some scholars argue that the fall of the Mongol Empire began upon the death of Genghis Khan. When he died, the empire was split up into four different areas managed by each of his sons. Ogedei, who was the third son, was given supreme leadership of the empire. Chagatai was put in charge of central Asia and northern Iran. Tolui, the youngest, received a small bit of land near the Mongol homeland. Jochi, the eldest son, who had died before his father, was given the territory that now makes up Russia. His son Batu would later form the Golden Horde in this area.

The empire was split. It would be affected by interfamily wars. Yet it would once again be united under the leadership of one man: Kublai Khan. He was a grandson of the great Genghis Khan.

CHAPTER 2

CIVIL UNREST AND THE RISE OF KUBLAI KHAN

Ogedei, third son of Genghis Khan, was a forceful leader. Despite the fact that the empire was split, Ogedei maintained control of the armies. His first mission was to continue the expansion of the Mongol Empire. In the first two years of his rule, Ogedei conquered northern China and Korea and expanded into the Middle East. In 1236, the Mongol army set its sights on conquering eastern Europe. Batu, grandson of Genghis Khan, led a campaign that swept through Russia with more than 150,000 men. The next step was to take over central and western Europe. As Batu's army was preparing for the attack, they were called back to the Mongol capital. Ogedei had died. A new great khan needed to be chosen. This may have been the best thing to happen for western Europe. The Mongol Empire never resumed plans for attack upon that area.

CHAOS OF ELECTION

As per Genghis Khan's order, when the great khan died, all of the leaders had to gather in the capital to elect a new khan. This was known as a kurultai. The transition to the newest great khan did not go as smoothly as the last one. Ogedei

Ogedei Khan was the third son of Genghis Khan, but because of his strength of character, he was chosen by his father to be the second great khan.

had chosen his grandson as his successor. This displeased his wife, Toregene. She was acting as regent, ruler on behalf of her deceased husband. Toregene wanted her son Guyuk to take over as great khan. Others, including Batu, supported Mongke, Tolui's son. Batu felt that Guyuk would not continue to expand the empire into western Europe. He felt that Mongke, who was more of a warrior, would continue the quest.

Although Mongke had the support of Batu and other members of Genghis Khan's family, Toregene got her way. Her son Guyuk was named the next great khan. The tension within the family increased during Guyuk's rule. This internal civil war was disruptive to the empire. Nothing much was accomplished for several years. Guyuk continued to war with Batu. Eventually he prepared to attack Batu's forces. Sorghaghtani, Tolui's wife and an ally of Batu's, told Batu of the impending attack. Before Guyuk could carry out the assault, he died. For a short time, Guyuk's widow, Oghul-Ghaimish, took over the rule of the empire. This was just until a new kurultai could be held.

Sorghaghtani wanted her son Mongke to be the new ruler of the empire. In 1251, he was confirmed as the great khan. The families of Ogedei and Chaghatai claimed that Mongke's election was invalid. A power struggle between the families took place. In the end, Mongke kept the title of great khan. Mongke's first acts were to purge all of his opposition, including many of his relatives who had voted against him. Mongke then declared his plan to renew Genghis Khan's goal to conquer the world.

Mongol women were quite powerful and were expected to maintain order in their husband's absence. A few like Sorghaghtani, were given territories to rule.

THE "QUEENS" OF THE MONGOLS

Mongol women had many more rights than women of other cultures at the time. Since the men were at war for long periods of time, the women were left to rule. A few of them, such as Toregene and Sorghaghtani, even served as regents of the Mongol Empire for a short time. Sorghaghtani was the wife of Genghis Khan's son Tolui. She was a very powerful woman. When Tolui died, Ogedei allowed her to continue to rule Tolui's khanate by herself. She was determined to see her four sons do great things. Her wish was successful, as three of her sons—Mongke, Kublai, and Ariq Boke—became great khans. Her other son, Hulegu, was named ruler of the Il-Khanate of Persia.

CIVIL UNREST AMONG THE FAMILY

Mongke and his brothers Hulegu and Kublai teamed up to expand the Mongol Empire. Mongke and Kublai began a war against southern China. Hulegu headed through the Middle East toward Egypt. Hulegu successfully sacked Baghdad and took control of Syria, Iraq, and Iran. His conquest was short-lived, however, when in 1259 he received word that Mongke had been killed. He withdrew his troops and headed back to the capital for yet another kurultai.

For a second time since Ogedei's death, the succession of the great khan was troubled by civil war. No one knew which of Mongke's brothers would be chosen to become the new leader. Hulegu was still in Persia and not in the running for the position. The main candidates were Ariq Boke

A DIVIDED EMPIRE

The Mongol Empire that Kublai Khan inherited was not the unified nation that Genghis Khan had created. The division of the empire upon Genghis Khan's death had separated the territory into four different khanates. For the most part, these khanates followed the rules of the great khan, until the time of Mongke's death. The civil wars surrounding the election of Kublai Khan as ruler broke apart the fragile alliances. The rulers of the khanates were not happy about Kublai's acceptance of Chinese traditions, causing further strife with the great khan.

Kublai Khan, despite disapproval from his brothers, embraced the Chinese way of life, as shown in the Yuan celebration of his birthday.

and Kublai. Unlike his brothers, Ariq had not set out to conquer more land for the empire. Instead, he had stayed close to the capital and become a symbol of leadership for the Mongol people. He was very popular in the court of the empire and desperately wanted to be the next great khan.

Kublai made the mistake of not heading back to the capital upon learning of Mongke's death. Instead, he pushed his army toward the northern banks of the Yangtze River. Kublai's victory on the ground was not popular in Karakorum, the Mongol capital. People felt he should return, as required by the kurultai. The families of Ogedei, Chaghatai, and Jochi sided with Ariq Boke.

Before Kublai headed to the capital, he held his own kurultai to declare himself the next great khan. Ariq Boke and his followers quickly dismissed his claim. They called him a traitor for taking on the position without authority. A civil war broke out between the two brothers. Kublai enlisted the help of his newly conquered Chinese subjects. He offered them a reduction in taxes and food for their hungry. With his larger army, Kublai struck out for Mongolia. His goal was to take the title of great khan from Ariq Boke.

A four-year-long civil war followed. It was clear that Kublai was the better warrior. His armies outmaneuvered Ariq Boke's, and he took control of the whole of Mongolia. Eventually, Kublai's forces trapped Ariq Boke in central Asia. Ariq Boke surrendered, agreeing to Kublai's rule.

In 1264 a new kurultai was formed. Kublai was officially elected the great khan. The honor seemed a bit hollow. The civil war had broken apart the great empire. The descendants of Genghis Khan were stretched far and wide. Many had perished. The Golden Horde in Russia and the Chagatai Khanate in northwestern China reluctantly acknowledged Kublai as great khan. Kublai's focus was on increasing the Mongol Empire throughout China and the East. He did not have much interaction with either the Golden Horde or the Chagatai Khanate. As a result, these areas managed themselves and never truly accepted Kublai's rule.

CHAPTER 3
SPLINTERING OF A GREAT NATION

When Kublai Khan declared himself head of the Yuan dynasty, the individual khanates began to separate themselves from the empire. The movement of the capital of the Mongol Empire to the center of China (the same site as today's Beijing) was seen as a betrayal. An uprising within the empire occurred. Kublai Khan was barely able to suppress it to keep control. The uprising only drove a bigger wedge between Kublai and the rest of the khanates. Ultimately, this led to the downfall of the Mongol Empire.

THE DISORDERLY CHAGATAI KHANATE

The Chagatai Khanate was established in 1227 under the rule of Chagatai, the second son of Genghis Khan. He was not chosen to be the leader of the Mongol Empire upon his father's death. Instead, Chagatai was given his own piece of land in central Asia to govern. A great warrior, Chagatai believed in the Mongol traditions. Genghis Khan made him the guardian of the Yassa, the Mongol code of law. Chagatai ruthlessly administered this law and executed anyone within his khanate who did not follow it.

The territorial boundaries of the Chagatai Khanate were constantly shifting. That was because the majority of the people who lived there were nomads. The tribal people moved from place to place, herding their animals. They did not have many major cities. The Chagatai Khanate was very rural and did not have a cohesive government. This caused many wars between the different groups within the khanate.

The main resource of the Chagatai Khanate was the Silk Road, which ran right through it. This allowed Chagatai to collect taxes from the merchants and tolls from the travelers. Still, it was not enough to fund the poor khanate.

Chagatai died in 1242 and was succeeded by his grandson Kara Hulegu. After Kara Hulegu died, there was no clear ruler. This caused many power struggles within the khanate. The leadership position was held by more than thirty different people over a period of about 120 years. The rapid change in rulers led to an overall disorder within the khanate.

In 1369, the Chagatai Khanate appeared upon the brink of collapse when a new ruler emerged. His name was Timur. He claimed to be a descendant of the great Genghis Khan himself. That was not true, but it did not matter. Timur raised a huge army and set out to regain the western half of the Mongol Empire. Timur, or Tamerlane as he is more commonly known, conquered Afghanistan, Iran, and all of Persia. He then turned toward the Golden Horde in Russia. He stormed into Russia and took control of the capital. Timur then headed to India, where he brutally conquered Delhi. Next he set out for Syria and west to the Aegean Sea. He was almost seventy years old, but that did not stop him. Timur attempted

Timur, one of the last major rulers of the Chagatai khanate, attempted to reunite the Mongol Empire through many brutal attacks upon neighboring countries.

A NOMADIC WAY OF LIFE

Mongols were essentially nomads. That means that they traveled from place to place. They did not build permanent homes. They carried their homes with them. While Genghis Khan used Karakorum as his capital, it was Ogedei who built the first palace there.

The idea of seasonal movement was supported by the people, too. Mongol farmers guided their herds across the country. They were searching for grass and water. The invading armies took down fences as they marched. They wanted to return the land to its natural state, free and open for animals to graze. As a result, the empire did not leave much evidence of its presence behind. Only a few buildings remain from the ancient times of the empire. The legacy of the Mongols is not seen in buildings but in culture, society, and religious beliefs

to retake all of China in 1404. Fortunately for the Chinese, he became sick and died in 1405.

Despite being mostly unstable in its history, the Chagatai Khanate managed to endure for several hundred years, much longer than the Yuan and Il-Khanate dynasties lasted. The Chagatai Khanate was considered effectively ended when Timur died.

Descendants of the khanate, however, continued to rule a tiny part of the territory called Yarkland until about the middle of the seventeenth century. Eventually, the descendants of Chagatai would become part of modern-day India.

Hulegu, a grandson of Genghis Khan, focused on expanding the
southwestern part of the Mongol Empire into the Middle East into

An Artistic Vision

The Mongols were known for being bloodthirsty conquerors. While that is somewhat true, as a society they also embraced the arts and sciences. In the Il-Khanate during the era of Pax Mongolica, the artistic abilities of its people shone forth. Beautiful textiles, pottery, and jewelry were created. Manuscripts of religious texts were illustrated with amazing detail and color. The use of paper and textiles at this time allowed for books to be transferred from one type of design to another. The Il-Khanate leaders in Baghdad decided to construct great mosques, palaces, and other buildings to signify their conversion to Islam. Many of these items remain today and can be found in modern museums.

The Controlled Il-Khanate Dynasty

If the Chagatai dynasty was disorderly, the Il-Khanate dynasty was the opposite. Its name, Il, is a Mongol word meaning "controlled" or "not rebellious." Hulegu, son of Tolui and grandson of Genghis Khan, was the first khan of the Il-Khanate. His battle campaign in 1256 consolidated the territory in the Middle East. On a map of today, the countries within the Il-Khanate region would include Armenia, Georgia, Azerbaijan, Iran, Iraq, and small areas of Afghanistan, Pakistan, and Turkmenistan. The Il-Khanate was sandwiched between the Yuan

Ghazan's rule of the Chagatai Il-Khanate was noted for the wide
acceptance of Islam within the region, a positive sign for the Muslims.

dynasty, controlled by Kublai Khan, and the Golden Horde, ruled by Batu.

Hulegu supported Kublai Khan's election as great khan. This did not sit well with his neighbors, the Golden Horde. Berke, third khan of the Golden Horde, wanted Ariq Boke to become the great khan. To express his displeasure at Hulegu's choice, Berke joined forces with the Mamluks from Egypt. Together they attacked the Il-Khanate. For the next three years, the two Mongol armies warred with each other. Eventually, peace was achieved when Abagha, Hulegu's son, and Mongke Temur, Berke's son, agreed to end the conflict.

The Il-Khanate was not done with war. Immediately upon ending the conflict with the Golden Horde, they were attacked by another Mongol army. The Chagatai warriors had crossed the eastern border of the Il-Khanate. They wanted to increase their own lands. Abagha fought them off. For the next several years Abagha attempted to expand his territory into the Middle East by capturing Syria. Unfortunately, he was not successful.

Upon Abagha's death, his son Arghun took over. Arghun was a generous ruler. The peace instituted during his reign helped to increase trade and strengthened business with neighboring countries. Arghun was followed by his son Ghazan. Ghazan's rule is widely considered to be the peak of the Il-Khanate era. Ghazan focused on promoting the arts and education. He constructed great buildings, created a central tax system, and encouraged trade. The acceptance of Islam allowed for it to grow and spread within the Il-Khanate. This was not a good sign for the Christians, Jews, and Buddhists in the region. They began to be persecuted. The mingling of faiths, however, also led to the mingling of peoples. The Turks began to move into the Il-Khanate, and Mongol traditions became mixed with Turk traditions.

There was much confusion in the Il-Khanate after Ghazan died. Family members began wars as they fought for control of the khanate. The rulers who managed to take over were weak and unable to establish any kind of unity among the people. Finally, a man named Abu Said came to power. He ruled the Il-Khanate well. Abu Said fought off yet another attack from the Chagatai Khanate. When Abu Said died in 1353, he did not leave an heir, so yet again the Il-Khanate was plunged into civil war. It did not survive but instead was absorbed back into Persia and Iraq.

CHAPTER 4

THE GOLDEN HORDE AND THE YUAN DYNASTY TAKE CENTER STAGE

After Genghis Khan's death and before the election of Kublai Khan, the four khanates worked well together. The khans of each region all felt allegiance to the family. They would support the great khan in his demands. They even had personal stakes in other khanates. For example, Hulegu owned land in the territory of the Golden Horde as well as horses and men in the Yuan dynasty. The other khans had similar interests in the separate khanates. The idea was to keep the empire united through its economic interests as well as by rule of the great khan.

THE GOLDEN HORDE

The Golden Horde was the most remote of all of the khanates. It was located the farthest from the Mongol capital. That meant that it had a lot less interest and oversight from the great khan. Initially, the area given to Jochi, eldest son of Genghis Khan, was somewhat small. Then Jochi's son Batu decided to invade Russia. He spent the next several years slowly conquering the

Byzantine-style architecture first became popular in Russia during the rule of the Golden Horde. Many cathedrals were built with domes and elaborate decoration, such as the Assumption Cathedral in the town

entire country. Eventually the region that the Golden Horde controlled spanned almost all of Russia. It went from Siberia to the Volga River to the Caspian Sea. Next, Batu decided to attack eastern Europe. Plans for an invasion force were made. Unfortunately, the death of the great khan Ogedei occurred. Batu had to leave for the kurultai.

Before he left, Batu set up his capital on the shores of the Caspian Sea. His brothers Orda and Shiban set up a separate khanate. Originally, Batu was known as the leader of the Blue Horde. Orda and Shiban were leaders of the White Horde. Collectively, however, they are all known as the Golden Horde. For the next several years, the Golden Horde warred with the Il-Khanate. They disagreed over who should become the next great khan after Ogedei. In fact, Batu sided with the Mamluks. They were enemies of the Il-Khanate. Batu became trading partners with them. His descendants did the same until Mongke Temur became khan in 1266 and ended the war.

Under Mongke Temur's rule, the Golden Horde experienced great prosperity. He strengthened relations with Egypt and Russia. He even made peace with the Byzantine Empire. Egyptian architects came to Russia to build new mosques and palaces. The Golden Horde maintained control in Russia. They attempted to expand into Poland and Hungary but were turned back. This period of peace and relative prosperity lasted until about 1341, when Ozbek, the khan at the time, died. After that, different leaders fought for overall control of the khanate. Civil wars erupted. No strong ruler was found for the Golden Horde.

KUBLAI KHAN, SUPERB BUSINESSMAN

Not only was Kublai Khan a great leader and warrior, he was also a very intelligent businessman. When he took control of the empire, he forged trade connections with Persia, the Middle East, and Europe. One of the best commodities of the Mongol trade was Chinese silk. Kublai Khan encouraged the manufacture and export of silk. He ensured safe travel for all merchants along the trade route. Known as the Silk Road, this unending road stretched across all of the Mongol Empire and southeast Asia and into eastern Europe. It was the main

continued on the next page

Kublai Khan played a significant part in the development of Ming porcelain. Today these dishes and vases are very expensive and highly sought after.

continued from the previous page

path for supplies into and out of the empire. He even set up a fleet of ships whose sole purpose was to transport goods to Italy, India, and the Persian Gulf. Kublai Khan also enjoyed pottery. He promoted its creation and sale abroad. He ordered that all kilns must be registered with the empire and taxed for revenue. To offset the taxes and increase demand, Kublai encouraged the potters to be creative in their craft. The result was amazing blue-and-white porcelain vases that became associated with the Ming dynasty.

Timur, of the Chagatai Khanate, invaded some of the Golden Horde's lands. He even captured the capital of Sarai, but he did not take control. The Golden Horde never recovered from this blow from Timur.

For the next hundred years, the khanate limped along, ruled by insignificant leaders and not contributing much to the empire. Eventually, the Golden Horde was split up into different centers of power. It ended up being absorbed by the Ottoman Empire and Russia.

KUBLAI KHAN AND THE YUAN DYNASTY

When Kublai Khan assumed the title of great khan of the Mongol Empire, he set his sights on conquering the Song dynasty in China. He took one hundred thousand mounted warriors and attacked Xiangyang. It took six years of war, but eventually Xiangyang fell. Kublai Khan had won. He had done what no other man had accomplished: he had united China under one rule. Kublai Khan declared himself emperor of China. He took on the Chinese name of Yuan. Kublai Khan knew that in order to remain emperor of China, he must embrace Chinese life. In order to accomplish this, Kublai Khan built his capital in what is now Beijing. He surrounded himself with Chinese administrators and broke with many Mongol traditions. This did not sit well with his Mongol relatives.

In taking control of China, Kublai Khan now ruled millions of people. The Chinese had been devastated by years of war with the Mongols. Large areas of the country were without food and water. The farmers had left their lands to hide from the Mongol hordes. Kublai Khan organized farmers into a group collective called a she. A she was responsible for reclaiming the land. They were also to help with planting crops, stocking lakes with fish, and digging out irrigation channels. Kublai Khan knew that a well-fed population was much happier and less likely to rise up against its leader.

Kublai Khan also reestablished trade routes. He encouraged merchants to exchange their goods with foreign countries. He set up security on the Silk Road. Kublai Khan invited scholars from other countries to come to his capital. Science, technology, the arts, and religion all prospered under the great Kublai Khan's reign.

DECLINE AND FALL OF THE YUAN EMPIRE

Kublai Khan did not completely forget about his Mongol roots. Over the years he reigned as great khan, he still focused on expanding the empire. He fairly easily recaptured Korea. Japan was a different story. Kublai was never able to obtain a foothold in Japan. He did manage to win a few battles in Vietnam but never took control there.

The fifty-year war was a time of great chaos and much fighting among Mongol khanates and Chinese. Many people perished in

THE PEASANT WHO TOOK DOWN THE YUAN DYNASTY

It may seem incredible that a simple peasant was the one who took down the Yuan dynasty, but it is true. Zhu Yuanzhang was a leader in the rebel forces. As a boy he had studied Buddhism and learned to read. This meant he was much more educated than the typical peasant. Zhu understood how to fight a war and win. He gathered other peasants together and created a small band of followers. That small band grew as they overtook more groups of peasants until he had a good-sized army. Then Zhu established his own government in southeastern China. From there he staged his attack against the Yuan leader. In 1368, Zhu was successful in getting Toghan Temur, the leader of the Yuan dynasty, to flee back to Mongolia. The Mongols never ruled China after that.

Zhu Yuanzhang, a peasant, led a revolt that established him as the leader of the new Ming dynasty.

Kublai Khan's biggest challenge came from one of his own cousins, Kaidu, a grandson of the great khan Ogedei. Kaidu formed an alliance with the Chagatai Khanate and Golden Horde against Kublai Khan. Kaidu encouraged the khanates to attack provinces under Kublai Khan's control. Many small wars took place, but eventually, both Kublai Khan and Kaidu died, and nothing ever came of it.

With the death of Kublai Khan, his grandson Temur Oljeitu took over. Peace reigned for a short time. Then Temur Oljeitu died. After that, successors of the khanate were rapid and weak. Finally, in 1333, Toghan Temur took over the Yuan dynasty. His rule lasted thirty-five years. While he was a good leader, his rule was marked by a massive earthquake, followed by a huge flood and famine. The peasants were extremely unhappy with the high taxes, lack of food, and forced labor. One peasant named Zhu Yuanzhang led the peasants in a revolt against the government. He was successful, and the Yuan dynasty was left in pieces.

CHAPTER 5
CHAOS AND DISEASE

The end of the Yuan dynasty ushered in a time of chaos in Mongol society. Rulers of Mongolia lasted for a few short years. They warred with local nobility who had decided to take advantage of the lack of strong leadership. Huge portions of the Mongol Empire splintered into separate eastern and western parts. The eastern part split up even further into the Outer and Inner Lands. Raids from local rulers into central Mongolia increased as small groups looked to establish their own power.

The single language that had been used across all of Mongolia was abandoned in favor of regional dialects. The nomadic ways of old were resurrected. Two main ruling tribes, the Oirad and the Khalkha, began a fifty-year civil war. The empire continued its warring tradition with China until 1571, when the current khan decided to sign a treaty, ending a three-hundred-year struggle.

Of the four original khanates, the Il-Khanate and the Yuan dynasty were the first to collapse. It is probably not surprising, considering that they were the two that were most urban. These khanates had established cities and encouraged artistic and economic growth. The code of the Mongols in the past had always been to keep moving and never put roots down. They were nomads. It was the most nomadic khanate, the Chagatai, that would last the longest.

Why Did the Yellow River Change Direction?

The Yellow River is named for the muddy, yellow-colored water that travels through it. The cloudy water is a result of silt or soil that is pulled into the river from the sides of its banks. The silt builds up as the river flows toward the Yellow Sea. The silt falls out of solution and drops to the bottom of the river. Over time, silt builds up and can even block portions of the river. This causes it to flood. Such a flood happened in the early 1300s. At that time, the delta, or land that forms from a buildup of silt, became blocked. The water had to find a new way to exit into the Yellow Sea. Thus, the river changed direction. This has happened several times since. Today, engineers help to keep the Yellow River delta from becoming blocked since they don't want to create another great flood.

The Yellow River is one of the main sources of water for China. When its path changes, great floods can occur throughout Asia.

NATURAL DISASTERS

If not for the natural disasters that plagued China in the early 1300s, perhaps the Yuan dynasty might have lasted for many more years. A great earthquake in 1344 followed by a massive flood devastated the entire country. The Yellow River, the most important source of water for the dry region, burst its banks. The water flooded vast areas of countryside, including the irrigation channels. All the crops were destroyed. The result was a huge famine that affected the whole khanate. People were starving. Yet the Yuan dynasty forced them to build dams and repair the dykes to hold back the water. It didn't work, as the river flooded twice more in ten years.

A year after the initial flood, a huge pestilence swept across the country, killing thousands of people. A drought began that lasted up to forty years. The Chinese believed that the natural disasters were a sign that the ruling dynasty was not in harmony with the land. The people were looking for a strong leader to help them out of this situation. Zhu Yuanzhang was just that person.

TRANSPORTING THE BLACK DEATH

Famine, earthquakes, and floods were not the only issues the khanates had to manage in the fourteenth century. During the

THE SIEGE AT KAFFA

In 1345, the Golden Horde attacked a small town on the Black Sea called Kaffa. During the siege, warriors began to fall ill and die. The plague was striking them down where they stood and running rampant through the army. The Mongol commander saw this as a perfect way to take the city. He simply loaded the dead warriors into his catapults and sent them over the wall into the city. He figured that the people within the city would die from whatever had killed his men. It worked—too well, unfortunately. Some of those citizens escaped onto ships and took the plague with them to Italy.

The devastation brought by the natural disasters and the plague weakened the Mongol Empire. It played a significant part in the downfall of the Yuan, Il-Khanate, and even the Golden Horde leadership.

height of the Mongol Empire, many different cultures interacted. Europeans ventured into Asia and met the ruler Kublai Khan. They brought their own goods and customs with them. The mingling of the East and the West was seen as a good thing.

The Silk Road served as an important pathway between Asia and Europe. This made it the perfect place for the developing bubonic plague to spread. The bubonic plague, known as the Black Death, was said to have begun along the Silk Road. It may have started in the tiny settlement of Issyk Kul. Issyk Kul

The Silk Road was not only a great place for trade, but also a way to transfer disease and death, such as the Black Plague.

had its death rate increase from about four people per year to more than one hundred dead in 1338–1339. The plague spread quickly along the lines of the trade route, killing hundreds and even thousands. Researchers estimate that the cities may have lost as many as 40 percent of their inhabitants. Some areas may have even lost up to 70 percent of their people.

The bubonic plague is usually fatal. It is characterized by high fevers and oozing black boils, thus the name Black Death. It is believed that the Black Death entered Genoa, Italy, in 1346 via a port in Sicily. The ship is said to have come from Kaffa, a city that the Mongols were invading at the time. Over the next five years, the Black Death would kill more than twenty million people in Europe, almost one-third of the population. The East was not left untouched. The devastating plague also swept through the Silk Road and across the entire continent of Asia.

CHAPTER 6
LEGACY OF THE MONGOL EMPIRE

The great leaders of the Mongol Empire conquered vast lands. Against all odds they unified the continent of Asia. They brought together people of all races, languages, and religions. Their methods, while seemingly cruel, were no more so than those of leaders such as Julius Caesar or Alexander the Great. These two men had also controlled huge amounts of land and people. The influences of the Mongol Empire are still present today.

RUTHLESS CONQUERORS OR VALIANT HEROES

Many people today think of the Mongols as bloodthirsty warriors. Their reputation is true in that scholars believe that they did massacre millions of people. Their brutal methods of war were well known and feared. Roaming tribes were held in higher regard than stable cities. Fierce leaders were revered and always obeyed. The culture of the Mongols was one of great honor and discipline. The leaders enforced all of these qualities and ideas in their people. Unlike other conquering armies, the Mongols did not leave behind a single language. Instead, the Mongols allowed their people to speak their own language and kept the Mongol language private. In the end, they did not leave a lasting peace or strong government.

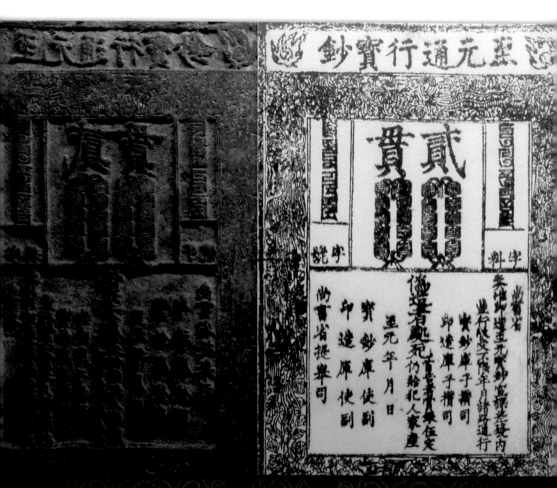

The Mongols took the idea of paper money from the Chinese and began to use it for currency along the Silk Road and into Europe.

Despite all of this, however, the Mongols did leave behind a direct effect upon the structure of Asia. The Mongol Empire was one of gigantic political force, bringing almost the entire continent of Asia under the rule of one dynasty. Many of the

MAPPING EURASIA BEFORE AND AFTER MONGOL RULE

When Genghis Khan was born, sometime in 1160 CE, his father was the ruler of a clan. He controlled about forty thousand families. At the time, that was a large group. It is interesting to compare the small size of the Mongol Empire at the beginning with the grandiose size of it at its peak—and the sheer numbers of people it took to capture all of that land. At about the size of the continent of Africa, the Mongol Empire in 1294 was between 11 and 12 million miles in area. At its peak, the empire contained more than one hundred million people.

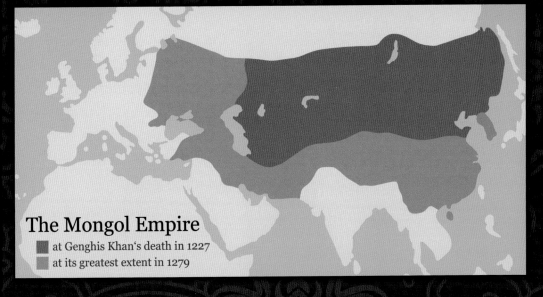

The Mongol Empire
■ at Genghis Khan's death in 1227
■ at its greatest extent in 1279

When Genghis Khan died, his empire extended from the Pacific Ocean to the Caspian Sea. His grandson Kublai Khan conquered even more territory to the south and west by 1279.

THE RENAISSANCE IN EUROPE

After the Black Death, Europe was devastated. Millions of people had perished. Much knowledge of the arts, science, and technology was lost. Many scholars believe that the Silk Road played a large part in restoring this lost knowledge to Europe. As a huge thoroughfare across Asia, the Silk Road was full of interesting people and information. Artists exchanged their creations. Scientific discussions took place. The flow of information from the remote parts of Asia and into eastern Europe was practically unstoppable. The Silk Road is believed to have contributed to the beginnings of the Renaissance, the explosion of art and science technology, in Italy and beyond.

countries unified by the Mongols, such as Russia and China, are still intact today. The peasant Zhu Yuanzhang, who overthrew the Yuan dynasty, became the first emperor of the Ming dynasty in China. The Ming dynasty ruled China for almost three hundred years. Under the rule of the Golden Horde, Moscow rose to power. It became the capital of Russia when Ivan III overthrew the Mongols. Ivan was named the first czar of Russia, and the czars ruled Russia for several hundred years.

In establishing strong rule, the rulers of the Mongol Empire served as examples for the countries they conquered. Russia and China both benefited from the Mongols' centralized government, some of which is still the model for today's administration.

STABILIZING AND PROMOTING WEALTH

The Mongols were the first to stabilize the trade routes. The Silk Road was the longest and most significant trade route of its time. It connected two continents and various other countries. Trade occurred on both land and sea and stretched for thousands of miles. The Mongols established patrols to keep them safe from robbers and thieves. This made them even more attractive to visiting merchants. In fact, when Christopher Columbus set out on his famous voyage of 1492, he was actually heading for the Silk Road. His navigation was off, but he was hoping to benefit from the goods that were being traded by the Mongols and Chinese.

The Mongols established effective and efficient lines of communication. They developed a mail system that aided the spread of communication and knowledge across Asia and into Europe. Paper was created in China, and its use spread along the Silk Road to Europe and beyond. The Mongols used paper money to conduct transactions with merchants. This idea for paper money had begun earlier in the Tang dynasty of China. The paper money that the Mongols used may have contributed to the spread of paper money in Europe years later.

Genghis Khan was ahead of his time when he ordered the creation of a written language. He wanted to be able to communicate with his leaders in a way they could all understand. That language was used until the twentieth century in Mongolia. The strong government and solid trade routes brought great wealth to the entire Mongol Empire. They spent money on medicine and technology and promoted developments in science and engineering.

SPREAD OF RELIGION

The Mongols embraced several different types of religions. They helped to further Islam's spread throughout Asia and the Middle East. The Mongols built mosques and used Islamic advisers to advise their government. The Islamic leaders saw this as a positive influence at the time. Mongols also practiced Buddhism, particularly the Tibetan form of Buddhism. They built monasteries and even used Buddhist monks to help them rule China. The Mongols also accepted a form of Christianity known as Nestorianism, which believed that Jesus has two forms, one divine and one human. One of the greatest legacies of Genghis Khan is the tolerance of many religions.

The Mongols should always be remembered as a significant participant in the creation of the world map of Eurasia. They contributed to the spread of wealth, information, and technology across two continents. The legacy of the Mongols continues in many different cultures today.

GLOSSARY

allegiance Loyalty to a superior or another group.

barbaric Extremely cruel or savage.

bubonic plague Also known as the Black Death, a fatal disease that spreads rapidly and causes high fevers, delirium, and black boils on people.

Buddhism Religion based on the teachings of Buddha.

culture A particular society or group and its beliefs in religion, the arts, and civilization.

dialect The unique way in which a certain region of a country speaks.

dynasty A line of hereditary rulers of a country.

famine An extreme scarcity of food that can cause people to starve.

Islam Religion based upon the Quran, a religious text considered by its followers to be the word of God.

khan Title held by rulers of tribes of the Mongol Empire.

khanate Individual regions of the Mongol Empire under the rule of separate khans.

kurultai A demand for all members of the ruling household to return to elect a new great khan.

nomadic Describing people who move around the country and never settle in one place.

Pax Mongolica A time of great peace and growth during the Mongol Empire.

qanat Tunnel system for funneling water to settlements and agricultural crops.

regent A person who takes over as temporary ruler of a country until a new ruler is elected.

ruthless Having no pity for other people.

Silk Road A trade route consisting of many different pathways extending from China to Eastern Europe.

steppes A large area of unforested grassland in Asia or Europe.

tribe A group of people connected by social and economic ties.

Yassa A strict set of laws created by Genghis Khan for the Mongolian people.

FOR MORE INFORMATION

Asia for Educators
Columbia University
116th St & Broadway
New York, NY 10027
(212) 854-1754
Website: http://afe.easia.columbia.edu/mongols/history/history4.htm
The Asia for Educators website of Columbia University hosts a wealth
    of information about the Mongols and their impact on world
    history.

Central Intelligence Agency
Office of Public Affairs
Washington, DC 20505
(703) 482-0623
Website: https://www.cia.gov/library/publications/the-world-factbook/
    geos/mg.html
The Central Intelligence Agency keeps a factbook of all of the coun-
    tries in the world, including their histories.

Exhibitions for Europe
Leeuwerikstraat, 15
B-3680 Maaseik
Belgium
Website: http://exhibitionsforeurope.com/genghis-khan-en/
Exhibitions for Europe has an exhibit of Genghis Khan that travels
    throughout the world.

Genghis Khan: Bring the Legend to Life
The Franklin Institute
222 North 20th Street
Philadelphia, PA 19103
(215) 448-1200
Website: https://www.fi.edu/exhibit/genghis-khan
The Franklin Institute is the most recent host of the traveling exhibit
    Genghis Khan: Bring the Legend to Life, which shows items
    from throughout the Mongol Empire.

Metropolitan Museum of Art
1000 Fifth Avenue
New York, NY 10028
(212) 535-7710
Website: http://www.metmuseum.org/toah/hd/khan1/hd_khan1.htm
The Metropolitan Museum of Art discusses the history of the
    Mongol Empire and also its effect on art and sciences.

WEBSITES

Because of the changing nature of Internet links, Rosen Publishing has developed an online list of websites related to the subject
of this book. This site is updated regularly. Please use this link to
access this list:

http://www.rosenlinks.com/MON/fall

FOR FURTHER READING

Abbott, Jacob. *Genghis Khan.* Akron, OH: Werner, 2013.

Baumer, Christopher. *The History of Central Asia: The Age of the Steppe Warrior.* New York, NY: Taurus and Co., 2012.

Beckwith, Christopher I. *Empires of the Silk Road: A History of Central Eurasia from the Bronze Age to the Present.* Princeton, NJ: Princeton University Press, 2011.

Chrisp, Peter, Joe Fullman, Susan Kennedy, and Philip Parker. *History Year by Year.* New York, NY: DK Publishing, 2013.

Craughwell, Thomas J. *The Rise and Fall of the Second Largest Empire in History: How Genghis Khan's Mongols Almost Conquered the World.* Beverly, MA: Fair Winds, 2010.

Donovan, Sandra. *Lethal Leaders and Military Madmen.* Minneapolis, MN: Lerner Publications, 2013.

Fitzhugh, William W., Morris Rossabi, and William Honeychurch. *Genghis Khan and the Mongol Empire.* Washington, DC: Arctic Studies Center, Smithsonian Institution in Collaboration with Odyssey & Maps, 2013.

Hyslop, Stephen G., and Patricia Daniels. *Great Empires: An Illustrated Atlas.* Washington, DC: National Geographic, 2012.

Iggulden, Conn. *Khan: Empire of Silver: A Novel.* New York, NY: HarperCollins, 2010.

McLynn, Frank. *Genghis Khan: His Conquests, His Empire, His Legacy*. Boston, MA: Da Capo, 2015.

Millward, James A. *The Silk Road: A Very Short Introduction*. New York, NY: Oxford University Press, 2013.

Outbreak! Plagues That Changed History. Turtleback, 2015.

Rossabi, Morris. *The Mongols and Global History: A Norton Documents Reader*. New York, NY: W.W. Norton, 2011.

Weatherford, Jack. *The Secret History of the Mongol Queens: How the Daughters of Genghis Khan Rescued His Empire*. New York, NY: Crown, 2010.

BIBLIOGRAPHY

AllEmpires.com. "The Mongol Empire." February 2007 (http://www.allempires.com/article/?q=The_Mongol_Empire).

Bio.com. "Genghis Khan Biography." (http://www.biography.com/people/genghis-khan-9308634#major-conquests).

Burgan, Michael. *Empire of the Mongols*. New York, NY: Facts On File, 2005.

Carboni, Stefano. "Heilbrunn Timeline of Art History." The Legacy of Genghis Khan. The Metropolitan Museum of Art (http://www.metmuseum.org/toah/hd/khan1/hd_khan1.htm).

Cope, Tim. *On the Trail of Genghis Khan: An Epic Journey Through the Land of the Nomads*. New York, NY: Bloomsbury, 2013.

David, Saul. *The Illustrated Encyclopedia of Warfare: From Ancient Egypt to Iraq*. New York, NY: DK Publishing, 2012.

Des Forges, Roger V., and John S. Major. *The Asian World, 600–1500*. New York, NY: Oxford University Press, 2005.

Dutch, Steven. "The Mongols." University of Wisconsin, Green Bay, September 1998 (http://www.uwgb.edu/dutchs/west-tech/xmongol.htm).

E-Mongol.com. "History of Mongolia: Chronology and Details." 1999 (http://www.e-mongol.com/mongolia_history.htm).

Forbes, Vivian. "Yellow River Changing Course." *China Water Risk*. ADM Capital Foundation, November 12, 2015 (http://www.chinawaterrisk.org/opinions/yellow-river-changing-course/).

Hansen, Valerie. "The Legacy of the Silk Road." Yale University, January 25, 2015 (http://global.yale.edu/content/legacy-silk-road).

History.com. "Black Death." 2010 (http://www.history.com/topics/black-death).

History.com. "Genghis Khan." 2009 (http://www.history.com/topics/genghis-khan).

Hooker, Richard. "Ancient China: The Mongolian Empire: The Yuan Dynasty, 1279–1368." World Cultures, May 29, 1997 (http://richard-hooker.com/sites/worldcultures/CHEMPIRE/YUAN.HTM).

Hosseini, Dustin. "The Effects of the Mongol Empire on Russia By Dustin Hosseini." The School of Russian and Asian Studies, December 12, 2005 (http://www.sras.org/the_effects_of_the_mongol_empire_on_russia).

Major, John. "Silk Road: Spreading Ideas and Innovations." Asia Society, 2015 (http://asiasociety.org/silk-road-spreading-ideas-and-innovations).

Marshall, Robert. Storm from the East: From Ghenghis Khan to Khubilai Khan. Berkeley, CA: University of California Press, 1993.

May, Timothy. "World History Connected | Vol. 5 No. 2 | The Mongol Empire in World History." University of Illinois, 2008 (http://worldhistoryconnected.press.illinois.edu/5.2/may.html).

McGill University. "Mongol Empire." 2009 (http://www.cs.mcgill.ca/~rwest/link-suggestion/wpcd_2008-09_augmented/wp/m/Mongol_Empire.htm).

McLynn, Frank. *Genghis Khan: His Conquests, His Empire, His Legacy*. Boston, MA: Da Capo, 2015.

The Mongol Conquest. Alexandria, VA: Time-Life, 1993.

The Mongol Conquests: Timeframe AD 1200–1300. Alexandria, VA: Time-Life, 1989.

Rossabi, Morris. "The Mongols in World History | Asia Topics in World History." Columbia University, 2004 (http://afe.easia.columbia.edu/mongols/china/china3_f.htm).

University of California, Irvine. "The Silk Road." 1997 (http://www.ess.uci.edu/~oliver/silk.html).

University of Maryland. "The Imperial Era: III" (http://www.chaos.umd.edu/history/imperial3.html).

Waugh, Daniel C. "The Pax Mongolica." University of Washington, 2000 (http://www.silk-road.com/artl/paxmongolica.shtml).

Weatherford, Jack. *Genghis Khan and the Making of the Modern World*. New York, NY: Crown, 2004.

Whitfield, Susan. *Life Along the Silk Road*. Berkeley, CA: University of California, 1999.

Wu, Annie. "The Yuan Dynasty." ChinaHighlights, March 2015 (http://www.chinahighlights.com/travelguide/china-history/the-yuan-dynasty.htm).

INDEX

ABOUT THE AUTHOR

Jennifer Swanson is the award-winning author of more than twenty-five nonfiction and fiction books for children. She has always loved history. One of Jennifer's favorite movies is *Night at the Museum* by 20th Century Fox, where they promote the saying "Where History Comes Alive." For Jennifer, learning about history or science is an active event, and she immerses herself in books when she is writing them. Whenever she is in Chicago or New York, she makes treks to the nearest museum to absorb all the history and science she can. You can visit Jennifer at her website, www.JenniferSwansonBooks.com, her special place to explore the world around her.

PHOTO CREDITS